F*CK LUCK, BITCHES

How to Start Betting on Yourself and Stop Leaving Your Life to Chance

BRANDEN LANETTE

Published by

www.SuccessIn100Pages.com

ISBN 978-1-947814-64-6
Copyright © Branden LaNette 2021

All rights reserved.

Except as permitted under the United States Copyright Act of 1976, no part of this publication may be reproduced or distributed in any form or by any means or stored in a data retrieval system, without the written permission of the publisher.

<u>LEGAL DISCLAIMER</u>:

The publisher has made every effort to ensure the accuracy of the information within this book was correct at time of publication. The authors and publisher do not assume, and hereby disclaim, any liability to any party for any loss, damage, or disruption caused by errors or omissions, whether such errors or omissions result from accident, negligence, or any other cause. If you apply the ideas contained in the book, you are taking full responsibility for your actions, and there is no guarantee you will duplicate the results stated here. Every individual's success is determined by his or her desire, effort, knowledge, and motivation to work on his or her business.

DEDICATION:

This book is dedicated to you, my reader. I see you. I honor you. And I'm grateful for the opportunity to share these pages with you. Now, back to work, because *fuck luck*.

WARNING:

Like my mouth, this book contains a fair amount of foul language. Put another way, I say *fuck* a lot.

I'm also known to throw in the occasional shit, piss, damn, hell, asshole, dickhead, and bastard.

Get over it.

Also, some people are offended by the term, *"bitches."* They find it disrespectful. I use it to describe an *awesome, assertive, empowered woman who wants to kick ass and get everything she wants from life and doesn't need to be saved by someone else.*

To me, this is the ultimate respect
and how it is intended here.

-Branden LaNette
(while putting on mascara and brushing the baby's teeth.)

Table of Contents

Introduction: You Don't Need
Luck, You Just Need You...   Page 7

PART ONE:
Is There Such a Thing as Luck?...   Page 13

PART TWO:
When You Wish Upon a Star...   Page 23

PART THREE:
You're Already Fucking Lucky...   Page 33

PART FOUR:
Beliefs and "Blind Spots"   Page 45

PART FIVE:
Lookin' for Luck in All the Wrong Places...   Page 58

PART SIX:
Paying the Price for Good Luck...   Page 72

PART SEVEN:
Try. Fail. Try. Fail. Try. Get Lucky....   Page 93

Final Thoughts: Be Careful
What You Wish For...   Page 103

> "*Luck is a dividend of sweat. The more you sweat, the luckier you get.*"
>
> -Ray Kroc, founder, *McDonald's*

BRANDEN LANETTE

INTRODUCTION

You Don't Need Luck, You Just Need You

Friday the 13th is a day known for bad luck. But you don't have to tell that to Henry Ziegland, also known as Hard Luck Henry.

The year: 1883.

The place: Honey Grove, Texas.

According to the legend, a man named Henry Ziegland dumped his fiancé, Maysie Tichnor, on the eve of their wedding. Maysie didn't take the rejection well, and in a state of utter broken heartedness, committed suicide.

This should have been the end of the story.

Far from it.

To avenge his sister's honor, Maysie's brother, Walter, in a rage, stormed to Ziegland's farm, pulled out a gun, and shot the man. Walter then turned the gun on himself.

Unbeknownst to Walter, Henry Ziegland wasn't dead. The bullet had passed through Ziegland's shoulder and lodged in a giant oak. Lucky Henry, unlucky Walter.

Twenty years after Ziegland literally dodged a bullet, the tree containing the bullet died, and he decided to cut it down. The job turned out to be more difficult than expected, so he enlisted the help of his son. Together, they hacked at the tree with axes for several hours, but the ancient oak was so tough, it was virtually impossible to split.

It was at this point the son came up with an idea: perhaps they could bore some holes in the tree and fill the holes with small amounts of dynamite. Exhausted and drenched in sweat, Henry agreed.

Once the holes were drilled, and the dynamite packed inside them, they lit the fuse. The pair moved 50 feet away and waited.

Boom.

As expected, the base of the tree exploded. What wasn't expected was that the bullet fired by Maysie's brother—which had been lodged harmlessly in the tree for over two decades—hurled through the air, struck Henry Ziegland in the temple, and finished the job. Can you spell Final Destination?

Fate? Bad luck? Justice?

Who the fuck knows?

The lesson I took from the story is simple: some things are out of our control. Shit happens, especially when we least expect it. The chain of events that led to Henry Ziegland's death could never have been anticipated.

Except for one thing:

They used dynamite to blow up a tree and only stood 50 feet away? How fucking dumb is that?

About the Title of This Book

I know what you're probably thinking: the title of this book is just a marketing device. Well, yes and no.

A good title that attracts attention is an effective marketing device, true enough. And I'm not above using tools and techniques to my advantage. You shouldn't be, either. But the title is more than that.

Fuck Luck is my way of saying, yes, luck is a good thing. And if you get some, great. But if luck doesn't show up? Fuck it. You do not need to be lucky to have a great life.

My definition of luck is:

- *A serendipitous, unexpected gift from the Universe.*
- *A positive result when the odds were against you (drawing the right card on an inside straight.)*
- *A better result than you deserve, earned or had a hand in.*

What Is Good Luck?

Brad Pitt gets lost on his way to a meeting with Steven Spielberg, accidentally walks into your living room, finds you utterly fascinating, and decides to make a movie about your life.

What Is Bad Luck:

Brad Pitt gets lost on his way to meet with Steven Spielberg, loses control of his Mercedes trying to avoid a squirrel, and drives his car through your living room wall.

What do these two things have in common? Both scenarios are completely out of your control.

Waiting for good luck to arrive is as ridiculous as waiting for Brad Pitt to arrive. Trying to avoid bad luck is as ridiculous as moving because Brad Pitt might drive through your wall someday.

You deserve to define your life on your terms. Don't be the victim of luck, either good or bad. Your life should be what you make it.

If luck wants to join you for your journey, pull over and let it hitch a ride in your car. But you should never be the one standing on the side of the road with your thumb out, waiting for luck to pick *you* up and take it where *it* wants to go.

The car is yours. You've got the keys. You're the driver. It's your life.

And if luck isn't there waiting for you when you get wherever you're going, well—fuck luck. Luck missed the journey, not you.

Success is not dependent on a lucky roll of the dice.

Wealth does not need to be inherited.

Health can be achieved by virtually anyone.

Happiness isn't something you find, it's a decision.

You don't need Las Vegas.

You don't need the lottery.

You just need you.

Bet on yourself every time.

The life I am creating for myself is not based on luck. Yours shouldn't be, either.

Luck is a nice thing to have, and it plays a role in my life, but it's a small part. I play the lead. The bigger role. I create my own luck.

But if the hand of luck reaches down to help you climb the tree of success, take it. But if it doesn't? Climb the tree anyway. Nothing is stopping you.

Most people think they need more luck. If this describes you, you've got it backward: Luck needs you. Luck doesn't show up—YOU show up.

Luck is waiting for *you* to show the fuck up.

Luck isn't looking for someone on which to bless its presence. It's looking for a partner. Someone to hold hands with. Someone to go along with on an adventure of discovery. Luck promises to be there for you if you do your part.

It also promises to abandon your lazy ass on the side of the road if you don't.

If you think you always lose, you will always lose. If you think you always win, you will win most of the time. Not always, but most. And if you're too afraid to play? Then you will just never know what might have been because you've given yourself the loss via forfeit.

Getting beat is bearable.

Forfeiting is unforgivable.

PART ONE

Is There Such a Thing as Luck?

From the bit of research my publisher required I do, it turns out that the word *luck* is from the Middle Dutch word *gheluc*, meaning happiness and good fortune. Shortened it's called *luc*.

You have probably also seen and even used the phrase, "As luck would have it."

This expression was first found in Shakespeare's, *The Merry Wives of Windsor*, circa 1600. So, luck has been around for a long fucking time.

And then you have a pot*luck* which according to my research literally means, "what may chance to be in the pot." Used in a sentence it sounds like, *"As luck would have it, Joan brought her special meatloaf to the potluck because everyone else was fucking lazy and got a quart of potato salad from the grocery store."*

One of the greatest scenes in the history of Hollywood movies takes place in the Clint Eastwood classic, *Dirty Harry*.

Dirty Harry has finally come face-to-face with the creep he's been chasing for the better part of two hours. Harry is standing over the guy, who is sprawled on the ground, and delivers his famous lines:

"I know what you're thinking, punk. You're thinking, 'Did he fire six shots or only five?' Now, to tell you

the truth, I've forgotten myself in all this excitement. But being this is a .44 Magnum, the most powerful handgun in the world and it will blow your head clean off, you've gotta ask yourself a question: 'Do I feel lucky?' Well, do ya, punk?"

This brings us to the question:

Is there such a thing as luck?

Well, is there, bitches?

Let's not drag this out. The answer is yes. Of course, there is such a thing as luck (duh) and, from my experience, it comes in six flavors:

1. Good
2. Bad
3. Really good
4. Really bad
5. "Holy shit!" crazy-good
6. "You've got to be fucking kidding me!" bad

Note: Any of the above can be served in a cup or, for an extra dollar, a chocolate-dipped sugar cone.

To make sure we're all on the same page, here are some detailed examples for each:

1... Good luck:

- Your best friend just landed a bartending job at the hottest club in town, and they offer to sneak you free drinks.
- Getting home right as the UPS guy is leaving your house after trying to deliver a package.

- Finding a $20 bill on the street.

2... Bad luck:

- Having it rain in the middle of your outdoor wedding.
- Having your refrigerator die right after you filled it with food.
- Buying a gift for yourself, then getting the same gift for your birthday.

3... Really good luck:

- You're up for a job promotion and the only other person being considered suddenly quits.
- The house to the east of you catches fire, but the wind is blowing from the west.
- Selling your shares in Enron the day before the company collapsed (somebody probably did, right?)

4... Really bad luck:

- After dying your hair blonde, you discover you're wildly allergic to hair dye.
- Getting your dream job and having the company file for bankruptcy a week later.
- Leaving your diamond ring at home on the day your house is burglarized.

5... "Holy shit!" crazy-good luck:

- Winning the lottery (not a scratcher, but the $100 million-plus Powerball).

- Finding a treasure map, and discovering the treasure is buried on your property.
- Going to adopt a dog at the shelter and finding *your dog*, who went missing two years earlier, sitting there (true story).

6... "You've got to be fucking kidding me!" bad luck:

- Surviving the bombing in Hiroshima on August 6, 1945, by fleeing to Nagasaki (bombed on August 9– also a true story).
- Cutting down a tree and having it fall through the roof of your house.
- Getting a death row pardon two minutes too late (thanks, Alanis).

If we agree there is such a thing as *"luck,"* we must also agree that some things are outside of our control.

Some Things <u>Are</u> Out of Our Control

I am a firm believer in the need to take personal responsibility for everything that happens to us, but there *are* some things we simply can't do anything about. Like?

- Where we are born
- When we are born
- Who our parents are
- The inevitability that things <u>will</u> change
- Government ineffectiveness
- The passage of time
- Traffic, accidents, detours, etc.
- The economy
- Pandemics
- An asteroid hitting Earth and ending civilization as we know it

- The weather
- Natural disasters
- Death
- Taxes
- The actions and feelings of other people

Wow, that's a lot of shit out of our control, and I've undoubtedly missed a few things.

This brings us to the question:

> ***If there are so many things outside of our control in life, why even try?***

It's a good question.

And here's a good answer:

> **Because there <u>are</u> so many things outside our control, we must exert control over the things we can.**

If we want the best life possible for ourselves and those we love, *we must control the controllable.*

What bothers most people *isn't* that there are so many things out of our control—what bothers us is when those things go against us.

- Born to rich parents? House out on Martha's Vineyard? Cool. Born into a family of poor goat herders in Uzbekistan? Not quite as fabulous (Note: this is not a knock against being poor, Uzbekistani, or goats, for that matter—but ask 100 people to describe the perfect life and see how many goats you get.)
- Born with Kelly Clarkson's voice? Fantastic. Can't carry a tune in a paper bag? Darn.

- Born to tall, beautiful parents? Score. Great genetics is a blessing.
- Living in a country with great leaders? Face it, no one gets this lucky anymore.
- Living at a time with no plague? Who would have known this was considered good luck?
- Finding your soul mate in kindergarten? Most people would consider this to be a big head start in the quest for love.
- Not getting hit by an asteroid is generally favorable (Don't laugh, it's happened.)
- Adopting a cat that doesn't scratch, bite, and comes when you call it? Bonus.

And on and on.

The point is: Some people get a head start in life. Others get dealt a bad hand.

Deal with it.

Or don't deal with it.

Won't change a damn thing.

It *is* what it *is*. The only question is what you decide to do from here. To quote Rod Stewart:

> *Some guys have all the luck.*
> *Some guys have all the pain.*
> *Some guys get all the breaks.*
> *Some guys do nothing but complain.*
> (Followed by a shitload of *"woo-woo-woos"*)

Complaining doesn't change a damn thing.

News Flash: Life Isn't Always Fair

This is one of the first lessons we're taught when we're young. Life isn't always fair.

- Put $2 in the candy machine and a Snickers bar is *supposed* to drop into the bin below.
- Work hard for eleven years managing the lawnmower department at Sears and you're *supposed* to be promoted into store management, not get laid off.
- Eat nothing but fruits and vegetables and you're supposed to get a clean bill of health, not cancer.
- Marry the man of your dreams and he's *supposed* to love you and take care of you forever, not run off with his secretary, Chloe.
- Get your Ph.D. in archaeological studies and you're *supposed* to live an exciting life, *like* Harrison Ford in *Raiders of the Lost Ark*, not end up working on the assembly line *at* Ford.

"What screws everything up is our expectations of how things are 'supposed' to be."

Wake the fuck up, bitches.

Fairness is an illusion.

What screws everything up is our expectations of how it's supposed to be. How things are *supposed* to work. And when there's a gap between how we think things are supposed to be and how they are, we become unhappy.

Disillusioned.

And part of us feels unlucky.

The problem is, dwelling on the unfairness of life doesn't make life better or fairer—it just fucks us up. Mentally. How? At first, when bad things happen to us, we think life is unfair. That we don't deserve it. But when bad shit keeps happening to us, over and over again, we start to think maybe it's us.

Maybe we're just unlucky.

And that's when things *really* go off the rails.

Once we start thinking *we're* unlucky, we start expecting bad luck to arrive. Then, when anything goes wrong—even the smallest thing—our belief that we're unlucky gets reinforced. Next thing you know, you're thinking you're one giant fucking bad luck magnet.

Dear Bad Luck,
Let's break up.

Dear Good Luck,
I'm available.

PART TWO

When You Wish Upon a Star

Time to go all *Disney* on your ass and discuss the timeless wisdom dispensed by Jiminy Cricket, also known by his rap name, J-Crick. Hey, if you can't trust a talking cricket, who can you trust?

Since his debut in the movie *Pinocchio,* Jiminy has become one of the great iconic Disney characters, singing Disney's signature song, "When You Wish Upon a Star."

Note: Jiminy Cricket in the movie looks almost nothing like an actual cricket.

This is what a cricket looks like:

This is what Jiminy Cricket looks like:

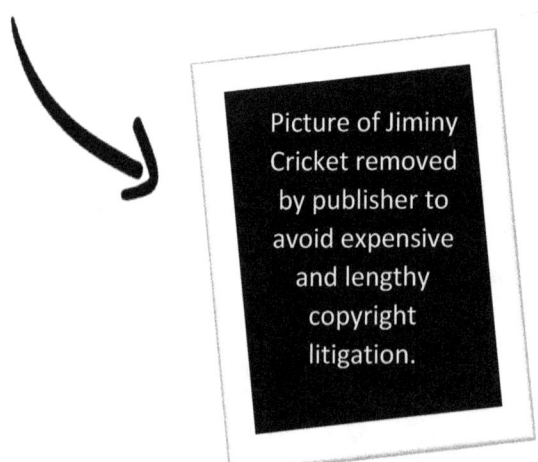

Picture of Jiminy Cricket removed by publisher to avoid expensive and lengthy copyright litigation.

I find the lyrics to *When You Wish Upon a Star* to be both interesting and revealing.

The song starts:

> **"When you wish upon a star…"**

My problem in the first line is with the word, *wish*.

What is a *wish*? Here's what the dictionary says:

- (Noun): *a desire or hope for something to happen.*

Bad start, as far as I'm concerned. Because I'm not much for *hoping* for the things I want, I'm into *planning*. I'm into *doing*. I'm into *making* things happen. Then, the definition continues:

- (Verb): *To feel or express a strong desire or hope for something that is not easily attainable; want something that cannot or probably will not happen.*

Wishing isn't much of a plan if you ask me.

I prefer the word, *ask*. In my experience, the Universe doesn't respond to wishy-washy-wishing. It responds to a more direct approach. As Tim Ferriss says, "Life punishes the vague wish and rewards the specific ask."

It responds when you *ask*.

Asking is the key.

The song continues with Line 2:

> **"…Makes no difference who you are."**

This is spot on. Nailed it.

I think it's fair to say the Universe is an equal opportunity provider. *Who* you are is irrelevant—and that's cool AF.

The third line says:

> **"Anything your heart desires..."**

I love, love, love this. The song doesn't say *some* of the things your heart desires. Or a *few* of the things. Or any *one* thing. It says *anything*.

Anything short of anything is limited thinking. The Universe is one badass motherfucker, so give it some credit, huh? As long as you're asking, *ask for what you really want*. Don't compromise. And never self-edit your dreams based on what you think you *deserve*. You deserve *anything* you want.

The only boundaries are the ones we set up for ourselves. The only blocks are the ones that we hold onto. You can create any life you want, and if your heart is truly in this, your request will match that.

Just fucking ask.

The 4th line says:

> **"... Will come to you."**

The song doesn't say, *anything your heart desires* needs to be picked up, that your stuff will be available at will-call. The Universe delivers. Think of it as Universal Door Dash. And it's free. No service fees. No $199 to join Universal Prime. Again, cool AF.

But the song isn't over. It continues in line 5:

> **"If your heart is in your dream..."**

Okay, here comes the fine print. You can have anything you want, but *some conditions do apply*. What conditions are we talking about?

The first condition is that that what you're asking for is something you really want—more accurately, something your *heart* really wants.

Advertisers spend millions filling our heads with lots of things we think we want, but they're not truly *our* wants: they are the things other people *want us* to want. No area is off-limits. Body, house, car, kids, pets, work, hobbies, travel, every area is targeted by all the world's big brands. You know, N*k* and C*ke and Appl* and McD*n*ld's. The barrage of messages from companies wanting to sell us something never ends. And with it, our list of wants grows exponentially.

> *"If owning a Lamborghini is what you want, go for it. But if it's not something you really want, the Universe knows the difference."*

Your Heart Should Guide Your "Wish List"

When we jam our wish list with gratuitous wants, the Universe knows we're not being honest and starts ignoring us. We become the little boy who cried, "wolf." Or, more accurately, the little bitch who cried, "Lamborghini."

Don't get me wrong: If owning a Lamborghini is what you want, who am I to tell you, you can't have one? Go for it. And I have no doubt if you want it badly enough, you'll get it.

But if that Lamborghini isn't something *you* really want, trust me: the Universe knows the difference.

If your heart isn't in your dream, the Universe moves on to someone else. Only ask for that which your heart truly desires. Your dreams are the connection between you and the spirit world. Dreams are the end goal for all the little tasks we have on our to-do list every day. Dreams matter. Everything else is noise.

Line 6 finishes the thought by adding:

> **"...No request is too extreme."**

That's right. No request is too extreme. But from my experience, no one gets everything they want. *No one.*

Think of it this way. The kid sits on Santa's lap at the mall (back when people went to the mall) and Santa asks (through his bearded Covid-mask), *"What's your name, little girl?"*

Kid: *It's Betty.*

Santa: *"Oh, that's a pretty name, Betty. So, what do you want for Christmas?*

Betty: *I'd like a Go Glam Nail Stamper, a Ms. Karaoke system with LED disco lights, a mini faux-leather backpack, a Designed-by-You Fashion Studio, a KidiZoom Creator Cam, a Nancy Drew starter set, a hot pink Barbie Corvette, a cashmere mermaid tail blanket, three scented unicorn-cupcake bracelets, a Zoe doll, and a Chromebook Spin 11 Convertible Laptop.*

Santa: *Are you done?*

Betty: *No, I also want a green Bibbidi Bobbidi Boo Bounce House and a 20-pak of velvet hair scrunchies.*

Santa: *Well, that's quite a list, Betty. And I know you've been a good girl and deserve everything on your list. But Santa's sleigh is only so big. So, of everything on your list, which is most important to you?*

Betty starts to cry.

Bad Santa.

Here's the deal: Santa is willing to bring Betty *anything* she wants—but there's no fucking way she's getting everything all at once. So, pick one thing, Betty.

You want the Barbie Corvette, fine, you can have it. But the whole list? *This year?* Don't push your luck, you greedy little shit. If you do, you might just find yourself on Christmas morning with nothing but a lump of coal.

The song goes on, and I have no intention of doing play-by-play for the entire thing, but there are two more lines worthy of review. One of the lines is:

"Like a bolt out of the blue..."

This is a great line because that's how we see success show up for other people—effortlessly, and seemingly overnight. Easy-peasy. What we don't see are the years of hard work it took for that "overnight success" to arrive. It's like watching a train pulling into the station without seeing the prior three days chugging down the track to get there.

Chances are good this is the first time you've read something I've written. You may even think it's the first book I've had published. It's not. It's my fifth. Might seem like a *bolt out of the blue* to you—but not to me. I've got 10,000 hours of writing behind me. All those tattoos you see on the cover—they're covering up a lot of scars of rejection.

Bolt out of the blue my ass.

Then there's the final line I'd like to highlight, which is:

"...Fate steps in and sees you through."

Ah, *fate.*

On one hand, I am a big believer in fate—events that are beyond a person's control (you did read Part One, right?) I'll even go so far as to say fate is determined by a supernatural power. But I also believe that we are in control of our place in the Universe.

Who Controls Our Destiny?

So, which is it, Branden? Are we in charge of destiny, or is our destiny controlled by fate? You may think this is a cop-out, but the answer is:

Both.

There are things outside of our control, *but we have enormous influence over the future through our thoughts and actions.*

> *"There are things outside of our control, but we have enormous influence over the future through our thoughts and actions."*

Some people assume if their lives are predetermined by fate, then why bother trying? They throw up their hands and say, *screw it.* Others believe destiny is completely in their control.

Here's what I believe:

I believe the hands of fate are on us all the time—guiding us, directing us.

But I also believe fate is kind *if you are kind.*

I believe fate is generous *if you are generous.*

I believe fate is benevolent *if you are benevolent.*

If you are caring, compassionate, fair, flexible, forgiving, hardworking, helpful, humble, passionate, patient, peaceful, resourceful, and tolerant, the Universe will respond in kind.

"Luck is not a business model."

-Anthony Bourdain

PART THREE
You're Already Fucking Lucky

You may have heard this little fable in your travels, and I have no idea who wrote it (Confucius, maybe?) but it's so perfect, I had to include it in this book.

Once there was an elderly, hard-working Chinese farmer who had one son and one horse. Together, they used the horse to plow the fields, grow their crop, and transport the crop to market. Without the horse, they'd have no way to make a living.

One day, just before planting season, the horse broke through the fence and ran away. When neighbors heard this, they exclaimed, "Oh, no, how will you till the land? This is so sad. What bad luck!"

The farmer shrugged and said, "Good luck, bad luck. Who knows?"

A few days later the farmer's horse returned, but the horse wasn't alone—he had brought two wild horses with him. When the neighbors heard the news, they declared: "You have three horses now! What good luck!"

The farmer shrugged and said, "Good luck, bad luck. Who knows?"

The next morning, because the new horses were wild, they needed to be broken. The task went to the son, who—while trying to mount one of the wild horses—fell and broke his leg. Now the farmer had one useable horse, two unbroken horses, and a son with a broken leg who could not help with the farm.

Again, the neighbors came and said, "Oh, how terrible! Such bad luck!" And again, the farmer shrugged and said, "Good luck, bad luck. Who knows?"

A few days later, the king's men rode into the village. A war had started, and they were enlisting the eldest son from each family to join the army and fight the enemy. When they came to the farmer's house, they did not take the son due to his broken leg, he was of no use to them.

As expected, the other farmers—each of whom had provided a son to fight—said, "How fortunate that your son had broken his leg. He alone was not taken!"

To which the farmer replied, "The story is not over yet, my friends. Good luck, bad luck. Only time will tell. Until then, who knows?"

We Don't Know What We Don't Know

Why are we so quick to label things as good or bad, when in fact we have no idea? Let's say I was running late for work. Then, as luck would have it, I spilled my Venti, extra caramel drizzle, extra whip, one pump honey Frappuccino on my fake-Valentino silk blouse and had to go back home to change. I was pissed off and carried that anger through the entire day.

But, what if...

I hadn't spilled my morning Starbucks fix?

I didn't have to go home and change?

Instead of being on time, I'd been hit by a semi-truck that ran a red light at Fifth and Main, and was sent to my heavenly father 50 years sooner than I'd planned?

What if the bad luck you've experienced was *good luck* in disguise? How many times could you have died but never knew about it? For all you know, you might be the luckiest fucking-lucky bitch on the planet because of what *didn't* happen.

We don't know what we don't know.

As author Cormac McCarthy said, *"You never know the worse luck your bad luck has saved you from."*

Our best good luck may have been bad luck. And our worst bad luck may have been the best luck ever. Take me, for example:

My "Bad Luck, Good Luck" Story

I wrote about this at length in *Once Upon a Time, Bitches*, so this will be the Cliff Notes version.

Simply put, my childhood wasn't good. I was rejected by my mother, went out on my own at the age of 12, and sued to become legally emancipated at the age of 15.

So, there I was, living on my own, got my GED, and enrolled in college to pursue a degree in criminal justice. I got arrested, changed my major to psychology, and worked three jobs to make ends meet.

I took drugs, became a foster parent to two young, troubled boys, got pregnant, got a divorce, and (wait for it, wait for it...) I remarried the jerk. Seriously.

To make sure you have the picture, I was:

- *A foster mom to two kids*

- *With a baby and a toddler of my own*
- *Taking classes I didn't care about*
- *With no prospects for a promising future*
- *Dreaming of being a published author*
- *Remarried the guy I'd divorced once before*
- *And with a third baby on the way*

Admittedly, my poor taste in husbands didn't help, especially when he had to cop a plea to a felony theft charge. I divorced him for the second time and (to save time, I'm fast-forwarding through loads of trauma), then I met my true Prince Charming,* a man who loves me more than any girl deserves, tattoos, stretch marks and all.

(*In full transparency, I reference my wonderful husband as Prince Charming here and in my first book, too, but please understand, he can be a royal pain in the ass at times and there are moments where I am seriously tested, but that's marriage isn't it bitches?)

> "As bad as some of what I went through was, I wouldn't change a thing. Not a thing. Not one fucking second of it."
>
> -Branden LaNette

So, why did I drag you through the story of my previously fucked-up life? Simple. To let you know that, as bad as some of what I went through was, I wouldn't change a thing.

Not a thing.

Not one fucking second of it.

Why? Because if I did, I wouldn't be where I am now. Married to the perfect guy. With six beautiful children who I would literally kill for (don't test me on this, I mean it.) And I probably wouldn't be making my living as a writer, speaker, and abundance coach.

The people who ran one of the proctor homes I was in as a teen used to listen to Tony Robbins and Zig Ziglar tapes in the car. The seeds that were planted in me during that time have played a big part in who I am today. Those seeds were worth all the pain. Pain has a purpose if you look for it.

One cup of unspilled coffee could have changed it all. That's a chance I would never dare take.

All my mistakes...

All the pain...

All the bad decisions and bad luck...

It was all exactly the way it had to be to get me to where I am right now.

It's a Wonderful Life, Bitches

Have you ever watched the movie, *It's a Wonderful Life?* It's hard to imagine you haven't.

The movie opens with George Bailey standing on the edge of a bridge, preparing to jump to the icy waters below.

Enter Clarence.

Clarence is an angel tasked with showing George what his town would have looked like had he not been alive.

In the end, George realizes that his life—even with all the bullshit he's been through, and the many sacrifices he's made—has been a wonderful one. He wouldn't change a thing. Suicide is off the table.

What most people don't know is that *It's a Wonderful Life* was not the original title. The original title was *The Greatest Gift*.

Sacrifices are gifts, even if we can't see it at the time. Pain has a purpose, even if that purpose is hard to see while we're going through it. And sometimes the worst possible luck *is* the best possible luck, if only we had a Clarence of our own to show us the alternatives.

What if everything that has ever happened to you in your life had to happen for you to be here, right now?

What if every setback, every ounce of pain, and every piece of "bad luck" was, in reality, a blessing?

Having my fiction stories rejected for 10 years was painful. But what if I was supposed to be rejected? Think about it: If I'd have gotten that million-dollar offer, I wouldn't be making the impact I'm making in other people's lives. I would just be one of the ten thousand authors writing fun fiction stories instead of doing what I do today.

Yes, there's more money being a successful fiction writer, but I'm not convinced it would be any more rewarding. Some people will say I'm rationalizing

> *"Bad luck for a young poet would be to have a rich father, an early marriage, an early success, or the ability to do anything well."*
>
> -Charles Bukowski

my failure. I prefer to look at it as rationalizing my success.

What if even the smallest change in your past—even something as small as a stubbed toe—created a chain of events that impacted your current reality? Admittedly, things might get better. But they might not. They could get worse. A lot worse. People you love, and who love you, might suddenly disappear. Would you take that chance hoping that maybe you could get an upgrade to first class?

Fuck, I hope not.

Most Problems Are *First-World Problems*

Want to take a sobering quiz?

No?

You're doing it, anyway. Grab a pencil and check the boxes next to the problems listed below that you have complained about (and be honest, because I *will* find out and I *will* hunt you down):

Your Problems Checklist:

☐ Spoiled fruit

☐ Slow internet

☐ Poor cellphone coverage

☐ Phone battery dying

☐ Television remote not working

☐ Misplacing your Air Pods

☐ The store is out of your size

☐ Getting a bad haircut

☐ Calls from unknown numbers

☐ Being put on hold

- ☐ Bad hold music
- ☐ A porch-pirate stealing your SodaStream cylinders
- ☐ Not being able to find the beginning on a roll of tape
- ☐ Airport security
- ☐ Having a runny nose
- ☐ Chipped nail polish
- ☐ Standing in a line
- ☐ Forgetting to bring a corkscrew on a weekend getaway
- ☐ A closet full of clothes but nothing to wear
- ☐ Blisters from a new pair of shoes
- ☐ Too much ice in your drink
- ☐ The air conditioner thermostat is acting weird
- ☐ Pulling a muscle exercising at the gym
- ☐ Uber being 10 minutes late
- ☐ Running out of hot water in the shower
- ☐ Too many junk emails
- ☐ Being charged 10 cents for a bag at the supermarket
- ☐ Not being able to fast-forward through a commercial
- ☐ The toilet paper roll is the wrong way
- ☐ Running out of toilet paper
- ☐ Having to walk the dog when you're tired
- ☐ Toilet seat left up

Okay, now go back and count up the number of boxes you checked, and let's see how you scored.

    ____ 0-10:   You are a lying bitch.

    ____ 11-15:   You're Mother Teresa.

    ____ 16-20:   You are an average complainer.

    ____ 21-25:   You are a true first-world complainer.

    ____ 26-30:   Get a fucking grip, bitch!

The truth is when we're thinking clearly, the majority of our "problems" aren't problems at all. They're inconveniences. They're annoyances. They're mosquitoes on an otherwise perfect summer night. And when someone points out something is a first-world problem, we can't help but nod in agreement because we know it's true. Three minutes later we're back living our *first-world lives* and complaining again.

The next time you find yourself complaining about a first-world problem, you should be ashamed of yourself. I know I am when I catch myself doing it. Which is still all too often. But I'm getting better.

You should, too.

When You "Bitch" Upon a Star

If it's true that the Universe is on our side when our thoughts and actions are admirable, then there's also the unavoidable flip side. When we're angry, critical, cruel, difficult, egocentric, greedy, and selfish, the Universe knows six ways to Sunday how to fuck us over.

If you are unappreciative of the gifts you've been given, don't be surprised if the Universe decides to hold up a mirror to force you to see the truth of what you've allowed yourself to become.

Trust me, you won't like what you see.

In short, the Universe is not arbitrary.

It wields enormous sway over your life, but it also responds and reacts to you.

You may not be in control of your destiny, but you sure as fuck play a significant role.

When you bitch upon a star, you get exactly what you're asking for: more of the shit that frustrates you, that makes you feel anxious and overwhelmed. You are going against the grain of the Universe.

This is what I call being, "out of alignment," and where you start finding out that misery loves company, and it's easier to bitch about your problems than it is to do something about it.

The Universe will match your energy, every single time.

"Are you placing enough interesting, freakish, long shot, weirdo bets?"

-Tom Peters, author, *In Search of Excellence* and *You, Inc.*

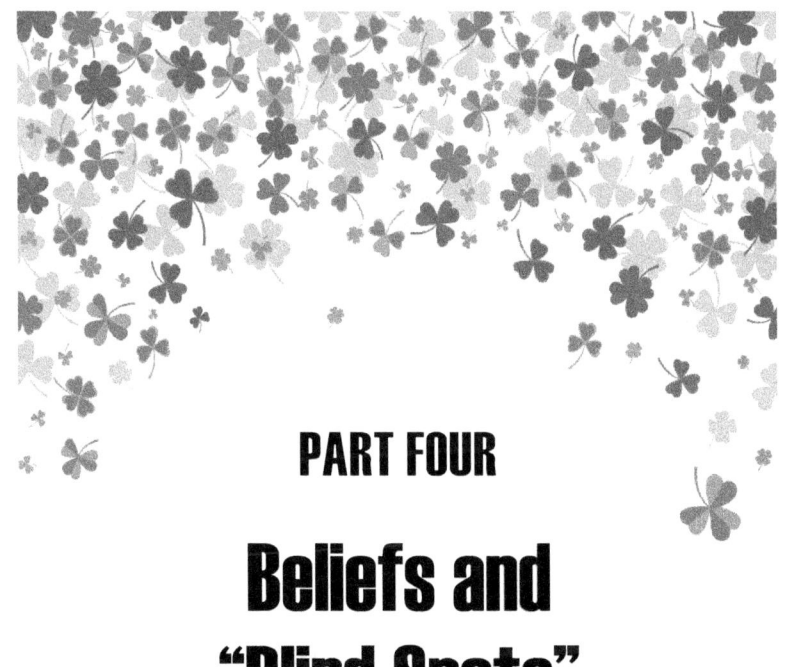

PART FOUR
Beliefs and "Blind Spots"

F*CK LUCK, BITCHES

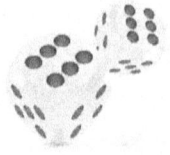

Are you superstitious? What superstitious beliefs do you subconsciously operate with? Like, don't walk under a ladder, or if you break a mirror, you'll have seven years of bad luck? Me, I never got into that stuff. Carrying the lucky rabbit's foot (does anyone consider how damn creepy that is—carrying around the actual foot of a sweet, innocent creature?) Or knocking on wood? Or throwing salt over your shoulder? I don't believe in any of that crap.

Perhaps you do, and I'm not passing judgment. Many people are super-superstitious:

- Soccer player David Beckham wore new shoes for every game.

- Actor Colin Farrell once offered a $2,000 reward for the safe return of his lucky belt—yes, belt—which he'd received as a gift from his father. (Colin also wears boxer shorts covered in shamrocks when shooting a movie.)

- Jennifer Aniston's ritual when entering an airplane involves stepping inside with her right foot first while tapping the outside of the plane.

- Keith Richards, of Rolling Stones fame, not only eats a shepherd's pie before every concert, he insists on being the first person to break the crust. Once, upon discovering someone had already cut into the pie, he refused to go on stage until a new pie was delivered, delaying the start of the show (much to Mick Jagger's chagrin.)

- Megan Fox says she listens to Britney Spears whenever she flies. She says it's impossible to believe her destiny is to die listening to Britney Spears, so she knows the plane won't crash as long as she has Britney on.
- Madonna wears a red string bracelet to ward off bad luck.
- For good luck, Michael Jordan wore a pair of his University of North Carolina shorts under his Bulls uniform.
- Serena Williams wears a special pair of socks that she says she's never lost a match in.
- It's said that model Heidi Klum carries a bag of her own baby teeth around with her as a good luck charm (yuck).
- Steven Tyler wears a necklace made from the teeth of a raccoon he caught as a child.

And, while most people believe 13 to be unlucky, Taylor Swift is in love with the number so much she paints it on the back of her hand when going on stage.

(Disclaimer: I have no idea if any of the above is true since I have never met a single person on this list. All information was uncovered during a standard Google search.)

Now, if you happen to be the type who believes in this kind of shit, I'd like to mention that if you write a positive review on Amazon, good luck will be your reward and $10,000 will magically show up in your bank account. Don't sue me if it doesn't. You were the gullible one, not me.

Where Does This Shit Come From?

Where do superstitions come from? How did they get their start? In most cases, superstitions stem from people's fear of the unknown. When we fear things which we can't see (for example, monsters and ghosts), our brains make stuff up to protect us. While I think this is silly, there is something to be said for believing in the unseen.

I believe in many things I can't see.

For years I believed I would someday find my Prince Charming, and I did. There *is* power in belief. So, if you want to wear a belly button ring made from Australian clamshells, go for it. Just make sure the shells are empty and dry. Nothing smells worse than six-week-old clams.

I also think there's something to be said for the idea of beginner's luck. Beginners are often too naïve to know they can't win, so they try, anyway. Lo and behold, beginners sometimes win, hence the moniker. I refuse to call it luck. I call it *showing the fuck up*. Amazing things happen when you show the fuck up. Nothing happens when you don't (we'll talk more on this later.)

Beyond that, most superstitious beliefs are complete bullshit.

- (Good): Picking up a penny
- (Bad): Walking under a ladder
- (Bad): A black cat crossing your path
- (Bad): Breaking a mirror

- (Good): Knocking on wood
- (Bad): Seeing a flock of birds flying from left to right
- (Good): Crossing your fingers
- (Bad): Opening an umbrella inside the house
- (Bad): The number 4 in China, Japan, and Korea; the number 17 in Italy; the number 39 in Afghan culture; the number 666 (enough said); and—if you're Gwyneth Paltrow—the number Se7en (*"What's in the box?"*)
- (Bad): Failing to respond to a chain letter
- (Good): Hanging a horseshoe over a door, unless it's pointing down, in which case it's bad
- (Bad): Unlucky birds include ravens, crows, magpies, and the dreaded albatross
- (Bad): Saying the word "Macbeth" or wishing someone "Good Luck" while inside a theater
  - (Good): Saying "break a leg" in a theater before going onstage (go figure)
  - (Bad): Tipping over a saltshaker

In some cultures, you should avoid pointing at a rainbow, throwing rocks into the wind, placing chopsticks straight up in a bowl of rice, and putting your shoes on a table.

Superstitious beliefs foster reliance on luck, rather than a reliance on ourselves. This diminishes our power.

Believing in superstitions is like sending up a distress signal, telling the Universe we're in danger. That we need help. That we need protection from bad luck. That we are out of control when we're not.

I believe *we* are in control of 95 percent of what happens to us. And if that's true, why would anyone focus an ounce of energy on the 5 percent that isn't?

You might play the lottery, hoping to get lucky. I don't blame you. I could use an extra ten million dollars myself.

> *"I believe we are in control of 95 percent of what happens to us. And if that's true, why would anyone focus an ounce of energy on the 5 percent that isn't?"*

Now, some people think that the longer certain numbers are not drawn, the better the probability of those numbers showing up next. This is mathematically incorrect. Lottery draws are *independent events* which means that every draw is unrelated from the one before it or the next one. This is the same for the game of roulette and rolling the dice, too.

I am no mathematician, so, we're not going to get into probability theory because I literally would've fallen asleep if I had to do the research. But I do know this: In any game, you'd like to win, *you have to play*.

Even the guy who got to heaven complaining to God that he never won the lottery got his ass handed to him when God said back, "Well, you never bought a ticket."

I think you should go a step further. Rather than just buying a ticket to your dreams, why not *be* the ticket?

Because you *are* the ticket.

Bet on yourself.

(Side Note: I buy scratch-off tickets and win all the time, which annoys the hell out of everyone around me. What can I say? Maybe I'm just lucky. Then again, maybe I *am* the ticket.)

The Lucky Number Test

kay, let's see how normal you are. Think of a number between 1 and 10. Okay, got it?

Then turn the page:

Did you guess, 7? Probably. Studies have shown that 7 is the most frequently reported as people's favorite number. Seven is everywhere, bitches:

- Seven colors in the rainbow
- Seven days of the week
- Seven continents
- Seven wonders of the world
- Seven dwarfs
- Seven deadly sins
- God created the heavens and earth in seven days (note: the seventh day was used for rest, which is only reasonable after doing all that work. Just think how much more he could have gotten done if he'd worked the whole week?)
- Seven is a prime number
- Oh, and I had seven "maxims" in my book, *Once Upon a Time, Bitches* (I didn't think of that until literally just right now.)

The main reason most people pick 7 is because it is considered a "lucky" number. Walk through any casino and you'll see what I mean. (It's the perfect bait and switch.) Everybody wants to cozy up to 7.

BTW: When asked to pick a number between 1-100, 77 is the second choice. The number one choice is 68. Go figure.

The point is that 7 has a mythical reputation, and we're always looking for signs of luck (which explains me saying, *"Oh look, babe, our Big Mac and fries cost $17.77. We should have gotten these for free!"*)

Our desire for luck is ever-present and never-ending. The problem is that most of us have luck *blind spots*.

Blind Spots

I believe being able to see things in your mind's eye is the first step in manifesting things and making them real. That's why part of my daily meditation includes visualizing my highest self, doing magnificent things. It's also why I dedicated so much time in *Once Upon a Time, Bitches*, covering the importance of vision boards, and created *The Dream Big, Bitches, Vision Book* as a tool for doing this.

While visualization is an accepted practice for most people, my work as an abundance coach has shown me there are still some holdouts. They think the law of attraction is simply wishful thinking. Made up. Some people have been so direct as to tell me they think it's bullshit.

What this says to me is that they have a success blind spot.

The classic example of a blind spot is when you're driving, look in the side mirror, and see nothing. Then you turn, glance over your 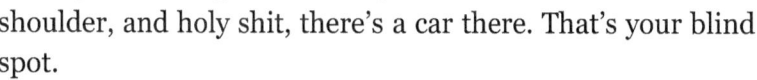 shoulder, and holy shit, there's a car there. That's your blind spot.

If you're a defensive driver like me, you go out of your way to avoid driving in other people's blind spots for that very reason—because you know they can't see you. This is what I call an *environmental blind spot*.

Physical Blind Spots

Most people don't realize it, but we have actual blind spots in our eyes. Don't freak out and rush off to the optometrist. We all have them. They're normal. Want proof you have a blind spot? Do this exercise:

- Hold this book out at arm's length and look at the dot and the clover on the page above.
- Close your left eye. You'll notice you still see both the dot on the left and the cloverleaf on the right.
- Now, focus your attention on the dot on the left. You can still see the clover, right?
- Keeping your eye on the dot on the left, gradually pull the book toward you.
- Keep moving it slowly toward you and there will come a moment where the clover disappears. Why? Because it's in your blind spot.

Cool, huh?

This is a physical blind spot.

Now, let's move on to the third type of blind spot—one that fucks us over without our even knowing it.

Opportunity Blind Spots

In the same way that we have environmental blind spots (the car you don't see in the rearview mirror) and physical blind spots (in your eyes), we also have what I call Opportunity Blind Spots. These are beliefs—or a lack of beliefs—that keep us from seeing the truth about what should be obvious. Here are what I believe to be the top three:

Opportunity Blind Spot #1:
A lack of belief in the Law of Attraction. (LOA)

This blind spot develops because you:

- Refuse to believe in anything that is even mildly mystical and/or supernatural
- Have tried applying the LOA, but you gave up too early

Opportunity Blind Spot #2:
You don't believe it because LOA is invisible.

You think the LOA doesn't work because you can't see it working. Which is ridiculous.

This would be like going to the car wash, then sitting in the waiting area with your eyes closed as they wash your car. Then, even though your car is now spotless, you refuse to believe the car wash washed your car because you didn't see it happen.

Everything you have in your life right now was attracted by you. Everything. And the LOA doesn't give a flying fuck whether you believe in it or not.

Or whether you see it at work.

Or notice it at all.

Opportunity Blind Spot #3:
An unwillingness to take responsibility for your life.

This blind spot occurs because you're scared shitless that you might be wrong—that the LOA *is* actually real—and that it's always been real.

If this is the case, then who would be responsible for everything that has happened to you in your life?

You would.

Taking the blame for what you've attracted into your life, and what you didn't attract, is just too painful. So, you turn a blind eye to the whole concept. Better to put your head in the sand than see the truth.

Then, there's the fourth blind spot. One that is also your fault. It is:

Opportunity Blind Spot #4:
You haven't told your brain what you want, so it doesn't know what to look for.

This blind spot is so important, I've dedicated the entire next section to it.

"Luck always seems to be against the person who depends on it."

-Anonymous

PART FIVE
Lookin' for Luck in All the Wrong Places

The luckiest thing that ever happened to any of us is that we were given a brain. The question is, are we smart enough to tell it what we want it to do?

When we make the shift from *wishing for luck* to *looking for opportunity*, we move from a state of reactivity to one of proactivity. In other words, we're no longer waiting for stuff to happen; we've given our brain a specific and targeted task we'd like it to complete.

Consider the following conversation between you and your brain:

> You (thinking): Damn, I'm depressed. Nothing is going the way I thought it would. And I'm broke. Life sucks.
>
> Brain: Well, let me help you.
>
> You: What the fuck! Who said that?!
>
> Brain: Me, your brain.
>
> You: Jesus, you scared the living shit out of me.
>
> Brain: So, you need help?
>
> You: Uh, yes. I guess I do.
>
> Brain: Okay, why don't you start by telling me what you want me to do.

> You: You don't know what to do? Fuck, no wonder I'm not getting anywhere.
>
> Brain: Don't give me that shit, I do a fuckload around here. I'm in charge of all five senses, breathing, speech, problem-solving, spatial perception, sleep cycles, balance...
>
> You: I get it, I get it. You do a lot. And you want even more to do?
>
> Brain: Yes. I'm capable of just about anything. So, for the third time, *what do you want?*
>
> You: Well, I could use some good luck.
>
> Brain: That's it?
>
> You: Yes.
>
> Brain: Jeez, why didn't you say so? Consider it done!

The next day, you're walking down the street and suddenly you notice a shiny penny on the sidewalk. You bend down and pick it up.

> Brain: There's your good luck. Anything else before I go back to monitoring your heart rate?

Okay, I admit the above conversation is ridiculous. But is it?

We all know the brain is one powerful tool. I don't think most of us use it one fraction as much as we could. Scientists say the brain has approximately 100 billion neurons with about 1 quadrillion (a quadrillion is 1 million x 1 billion) connections known as synapses that wire everything together.

These neurons are like relay stations for electrical signals, and blah, blah, blah…

Let's cut to the chase, shall we?

The human brain doesn't just *act* like a computer, it *is* a computer—more powerful than any computer that will ever exist. Ever. And what are we doing with it? We're sending it out for milk.

The brain wants to do extraordinary shit, and we ask for virtually nothing. We put it on autopilot—doing some very important shit, no doubt—but it's capable of so much more. It wants to be challenged, and we're asking it to find something to watch on Netflix.

(BTW: Did you see the last season of *Outlander?* I just adore this show, not to mention Jamie's abs. What? You've never watched *Outlander?* You're missing the best show ever!)

The Reticular Activating System

How do we tell our brain what to look for, other than just pennies? The answer is the Reticular Activating System, also known as the RAS.

The RAS is a network of brain cells and neurons located in the brain stem whose main job is to control sleep and the fight-or-flight response.

Have you ever fallen to sleep with the TV on? Or with the stereo playing? Or with your significant other droning on about their rough day?

Of course, you have.

What's interesting is that—even though the sound of the TV or stereo or the other person's voice continues, even loudly, perhaps—your conscious brain turns the sound off and lets you fall asleep.

Weird, huh?

No, here's what's weird:

Even though your brain has muted the sound of the TV, etc., *it's still listening*. Listening for what? It's listening for things that are important to you. Like what?

Like a knock at the door.

Or your child crying.

Or the alarm clock going off in the morning, so you don't get fired from your job.

This is the RAS in action. It is constantly using all five senses to detect anything around it thinks may be important. Like glass breaking downstairs when you're sleeping, which may be an intruder. Like lights flashing at a railroad crossing, to warn you about a train. Like the sound of branches crackling in the woods, which might be a wild animal. Like the smell of smoke because there might be a fire—or bacon.

Here's a classic example of the RAS in action:

You're walking through the airport, trying to get to your gate through a throng of people talking, suitcase wheels whirring, boarding announcements blaring overhead, all while you're having a conversation with your travel partner about whether they packed deodorant. Then suddenly, out of nowhere, you hear…

Your name.

Wait. Did someone say *my name?*

Then, you hear it again: *Branden LaNette, please return to airport security to retrieve a personal item. Branden LaNette, please return to airport security.*

That's your RAS doing its job, paying attention to anything it thinks might be important to you.

Let's just say that the RAS is your BFF. It's like having ADT but without paying for installation and the monthly fee. But that's not all. Here's where things get *really* exciting:

You can program the RAS in terms of what you want it to pay attention to.

And this is fucking awesome!

Why?

Think about it. What if instead of simply having your brain trying to keep you from danger, what if you could program it to look for opportunities? Opportunities to get what you want. To be more successful. To meet the right person. To make more money. To be luckier. *Well, you can.*

How do I know?

Because I do it all the time.

When the Student Is Ready...

There is a saying, most often attributed to Buddha, that goes: *When the student is ready, the teacher will appear.* I'm sure you've heard it.

Without question, it's one of the most famous, Zen, Namaste-inspiring, *"sound of one hand clapping"* sayings of all time.

The problem is, it's wrong.

Not to take a shit on Buddha, but what the saying *should* be is:

> **When the student is ready, the student will finally notice the teacher who has been there the entire time.**

For years you've thought about learning to play the guitar. One day, you see there's a sale on guitars starting Saturday. You go to the store and buy one. You take it home with a learn-the-guitar book and try to teach yourself to play it. You suck. If only you knew someone who knew how to play, someone who could teach you.

The next day, a friend from work comes over to watch the big game and he sees your guitar leaning against the wall. "I didn't know you played the guitar," he says. "I don't," you say. "Do you?"

"Hell, yeah," he says. "Been playing since I was twelve. I can teach you if you want."

This is unbelievable, you think. I buy a guitar and out of nowhere, a teacher appeared. The saying is true!

But that's not what happened. Is it? The teacher didn't appear. They were there all along, hiding in plain sight. In reality, there are probably ten people around you who could be teachers. They didn't just *appear*. They were always there.

Back to That Lucky Penny

Do you really think, because you wanted to find a penny, the Universe stopped what it was doing and tossed a penny on the sidewalk so you could find it? No. The Universe is busy doing Universe-level shit, not placing pennies like the Easter Bunny hiding eggs.

Consider this:

There's a guy in Florida who developed the habit of looking for lost change during his daily four-hour walk during which he feeds stray cats (nice guy, huh?) Want to guess how much change he finds? $5.60 per day.

Over 10 years, he found $21,495 in lost change, which he donated to a local animal rescue (we're talking *really* nice guy, now.) And this is not a one-off example.

A family in New York picked up pennies and other coins dropped on sidewalks and put them in a jar. At the end of the year, they had $1,013.

How much lost money is lying around? No one knows. The U.S. Mint once estimated that as much as $3 billion in change ends up on sidewalks or slipping between sofa cushions. And let's not even get started on printed bills.

The fact is, we step right over lost change every day without ever noticing. Why? Because we're not looking for it. Our priorities and our attention are elsewhere.

When you start looking for pennies, you start seeing them everywhere.

If you really believe you will find a penny on the street, then you will. And when you do, hold the penny in your hand and yourself: *Is this penny in my hand because of luck, or because I made a conscious decision to look for one?*

You know the answer.

How many pennies (or quarters, or dollars) have you stepped over in your life because you didn't tell your mind to look for them? How many opportunities have you missed for the same reason?

Look for bad luck, and sure as fuck, you'll find some.

Look for good luck, and…

(*…you can finish the sentence for yourself.*)

The Strangest Secret

In 1956, a man named Earl Nightingale made a 19-minute record called, *The Strangest Secret*. The recording sold an astounding one million copies and received the first Gold Record ever awarded for the spoken word. Even more, this recording launched the world of motivation and audio publishing as we know it today.

So, what is the strangest secret? According to Nightingale, the strangest secret is:

> *"You become what you think about."*

I have my version, which goes like this:

> *"What I become will be what I think about, and what I say to myself."*

Not living the life you want? *What have you been thinking about and saying to yourself?*

Not having enough good luck? *What have you been thinking about and saying to yourself?*

Too much bad luck manifesting itself in your life? *Yeah, same thing.*

It makes me crazy when I see otherwise intelligent people complain about the sad state of their lives when the very act of complaining about it *is the reason.*

I challenge you to ask yourself: *What have I been thinking about and telling myself for the last six weeks? The last six months? The last six years? The last sixteen?*

If your life is not on track, I'll bet you my dollars to your donuts that your thoughts and your self-talk are the reason.

The world we manifest is a direct reflection of those two things.

Thoughts. And self-talk.

The things other people say to us have power, but not nearly as much as the things we say to ourselves. Tell your brain what you want, then watch in amazement as the opportunities to get them begin to appear.

Use Your Brain and Look in the Right Places

Willie Sutton was famous for two things. The first was robbing banks for over $2 million. The second was when asked why he robbed banks, he replied: "*Because that's where the money is.*"

Smart.

I think it's fair to say that Sutton increased his luck by looking for money in the right places. What's amazing is how many people claim luck never finds them, but what have they done to be in the right place?

In the 1960s, tons of musicians hung out at Joni Mitchell's house in Laurel Canyon. The Eagles, the Mamas and the Papas, Carole King, Roger McGuinn, and many others met and wrote some of their biggest hits there.

It was while sitting on Joni's sofa that Stephen Stills and Graham Nash discovered they could harmonize together. How lucky is that?

They learned from each other. They formed bands with the people they met there. They did drugs together there (not a recommendation, just a fact.)

But it's not luck at all. They *put* themselves there to *be* lucky. They were smart enough to know luck wasn't going to come to them. They were going to have to make their own luck.

They moved *to* their luck.

When asked why she lived on Lookout Mountain in Los Angeles, Joni Mitchell said:

> *"Ask anyone in America where the craziest people live, and they'll tell you California. Ask anyone in California where the craziest people live, and they'll say, Los Angeles. Ask anyone in Los Angeles where the craziest people live, and they'll tell you Hollywood. Ask anyone in Hollywood where the craziest people live, and they'll say Laurel Canyon. And ask anyone in Laurel Canyon where the craziest people live, and they'll say Lookout Mountain. So, I bought a house on Lookout Mountain."*

The Luck of Proximity

In an interview, Leonardo DiCaprio said he was lucky to have been born in Los Angeles, in the proximity of the film industry, within driving distance of Hollywood. *"I probably wouldn't be doing this for a living if I lived in any other location."*

What do Marilyn Monroe, Bradley Cooper, Julia Roberts, Dustin Hoffman, Jill Clayburgh, Marlo Brando, Jane Fonda, and Al Pacino have in common? They all got their start at *The Actor's Studio* in New York. You mean they didn't just get lucky? No. They studied and learned and networked and auditioned—*then* they got lucky.

You want to become an actor, but you weren't lucky enough to be born down the street from Leo? Call Two Men and a Truck. Fucking move.

Get on a damn bus.

Want to get lucky and meet a movie producer? Get a job waiting tables at the Polo Lounge and the next time Martin Scorsese comes in, give him your script when you hand him his check.

Want to get a lucky break in tech, move to Austin or Silicon Valley. Want to get a lucky break catching beaded necklaces, move to New Orleans. Want to get a lucky break in country music, move to Nashville. Want to get a lucky break and land a job as a blackjack dealer, move to Las Vegas.

Meet people.

Hang the fuck out in the right places.

Network.

According to the theory called the *Six Degrees of Separation*, every person on Earth is only six contacts away from anyone they want to connect with.

Let's say you want to meet Jack Nicholson. Ask yourself: Who is the most connected person I know? Not the richest, necessarily, but the person with the greatest number of friends, colleagues, business associates, etc. Your Uncle Fred? Okay. Call Uncle Fred and ask him if he knows anyone who might be able to get you to Jack. He says, "Well, the most well-connected person I know is my friend, Sheila Smith, who works in advertising. I'll ask her if she knows anyone."

And so on.

Theoretically, it should only take six levels of contacts to finally get to Jack.

Six handshakes.

Six introductions.

Six emails.

Connections are everything. The more people you meet, the more people you befriend, the more connected you are, the luckier you get.

Just ask Kevin Bacon.

"I feel that luck is preparation meeting opportunity."

-Oprah Winfrey

PART SIX
Paying the Price for Good Luck

I know what you're probably thinking: Branden, why would someone ever have to *pay a price* for good luck? Luck is supposed to be free. That's why we wish for it! Because we don't have to do anything for it. Right?

Well, yes and no.

Sometimes luck is free. You're just sitting there, minding your own business, and bang! It just shows up. A completely random event in which you had no involvement; total, unexpected, uncontrollable luck. Yes, it happens. A lot. But that's not what this book is about. It's about influencing your luck through your actions, and sometimes your non-actions. This is the luck *you* contribute to.

It's called karma.

At its most basic level, karma can be defined as: *"Getting back what you put out."*

You want good luck?

Then pay the price for it.

There is no question in my mind that what *goes around comes around*. It may not always be fair, and it may not come around for a long fucking time, or in the exact proportions you *think* it should.

Every now and then the Universe screws up and drops *your* good luck package on your asshole neighbor's porch. But, if you're honest, you know that your neighbor's luck ended up on your porch a few times, too.

The "Pay the Price" Formula

If there was a way to scientifically create good luck in a lab, I think the result would be the following "Four Leaf Clover" formula:

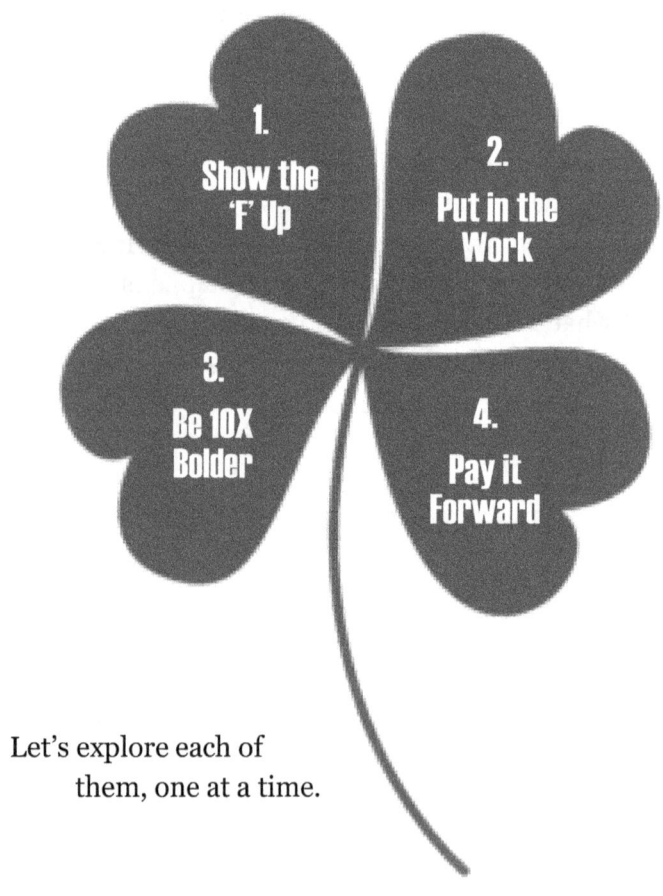

1. Show the 'F' Up
2. Put in the Work
3. Be 10X Bolder
4. Pay it Forward

Let's explore each of them, one at a time.

Show the 'F' Up.

While I can't claim to be a Woody Allen fan, I am a firm believer in his famous quote that says:

Eighty percent of success is showing up.

We hear a lot about actors who have to endure rejection after rejection. What we don't hear as often is about the roles they got that they didn't audition for.

- Betty White showed up to audition for the role of Blanche Devereaux in *Golden Girls,* but the role went to Rue McClanahan. To her surprise, they offered her the role of Rose. That was lucky.

- Heath Ledger showed up to audition for the role of Bruce Wayne in Christopher Nolan's *Batman: The Dark Knight*. He didn't get it, but Nolan thought Ledger was perfect for a different role. "Any interest in playing the Joker?" Fuck, yeah.

    BTW: Ledger ended up winning a posthumous Oscar for the performance.

- Sandra Oh was on her way to audition for the TV drama, *Grey's Anatomy,* when she realized she'd left her wallet and phone at home. She got to the audition feeling so rattled and nervous, she left early. Didn't matter. They offered her the role anyway.

- Ashley Greene auditioned for the role of Bella Swan in *Twilight*. Unfortunately, she was up against Kristen Stewart, who also showed up.

Stewart got the role. Greene was bummed. Then the phone rang. "Any interest in playing Alice?"

- Can you imagine anyone other than Matthew Broderick playing the role of Ferris Bueller? John Hughes could. The role was expected to go to Johnny Depp, who had a reputation for playing quirky characters. Fortunately for Broderick, Depp had scheduling conflicts.

- Miley Cyrus auditioned to play Lilly Truscott in *Hannah Montana*. She lost it to Emily Osborne, but it wasn't all bad; she got the lead role, instead.

- When Brie Larson got a phone call, asking if she wanted to have lunch with Amy Schumer and Judd Apatow, she had no idea she was auditioning for a movie. She showed up for salad and ended up with a critical stepping-stone in her career.

In a way, life is one big audition, regardless of what we do. We're *always* auditioning for something, whether we realize it or not.

Job interviews are *auditions*.

Networking events are *auditions*.

Dates are *auditions*.

Cocktail parties are great opportunities to finally wear that cute black dress hanging lonely in the closet, but they're also *auditions* for opportunities we don't even know about.

Your kid's soccer practice isn't just soccer practice—it's also an *audition* for parent of the year.

Life is just one big open call. The big question is:

Are you going to show up and be considered for whatever the role may be?

Showing up means stepping into our truest selves, acknowledging we are more than temporary forms of walking meat, and that our lives have meaning and purpose.

People who are living lives of meaning and purpose show the fuck up!

Showing up means changing the habits that put you into your highest power. Taking care of yourself.

Showing up means committing to healing your inner child as you step into the habits of the person you want to become.

Showing up means facing our fears and taking chances.

I know that if I don't show up, the lessons of life are going to keep coming and I'm going to keep repeating my mistakes until I get my shit together.

There was a time when I was in a serious relationship with alcohol. I soaked everything in it, including my liver. I was drinking for the wrong reasons, mostly to avoid feeling things, to numb myself. It was not a healthy relationship.

I knew that if I wanted things to change, *I* had to change.

I didn't feel lucky, I didn't feel like things were working out for me. I traded the habit for a different one. I'm creating that. Now everything is falling into place for me because I made a choice. I'm not leaving it to chance, I'm not sitting on the couch just wishing, hoping, or praying.

The Universe will always work for you if you show up and work for yourself. Change your energy, trade your habits, stop looking for the outside source to feel good.

You are the source.

If you're showing up and you're being your best self, outside sources are going to put everything in alignment for you.

Get in the Habit of Saying "Yes"

I love Richard Branson. Not because he's a self-made billionaire (though I *do* find that attractive in a man) or because he's hunky (I've already got my hunk.) What I'm drawn to is his habit of saying "yes" to things, in both his business and personal life.

"Even if I have no idea where I'm going or how to get there, I prefer to say yes, instead of no," he wrote on his blog. And he added one of my favorite mantras:

"Opportunity favours the bold."

> *"I've probably said yes too many times in my life, but I don't regret a thing."*
>
> -Richard Branson

(Notice the extra letter "u" in favo*u*r? Very sexy.)

Richard's position (yes, we're on a first-name basis) is that if somebody offers you an opportunity, even if you don't think you can do it, you should say, "yes."

"You can learn how to do it later!" he says.

A great example of his willingness to say "yes" came when one of his employees presented the idea of starting a low-cost airline in Australia. Even though he knew nothing about the airline industry he said "yes" to the idea.

Does saying "yes" create risks? Of course. But the risks are often worth the rewards. As Richard said to me one night over cocktails at the Four Seasons, "I've probably said yes too many times in my life, Branden, but I don't regret a thing," as he offered me an olive from his martini. Then he smiled and said, "Life is a lot more fun when you say yes."

I'm sorry, that never happened. Just me daydreaming.

An Entire "Year of Yes"

Another very successful person who has come to learn the power of "yes" is ABC's queen of TV, Shonda Rhimes, the writer/creator of *Grey's Anatomy* and *Scandal*.

When did she become a "yes" person? It was during Thanksgiving a few years ago when her sister, Delores, said, "Hey, pass me the gravy." No, what Delores really said was, "You know, Shonda, you never say yes to anything."

That got Shonda's attention because she knew it was true. As successful as she was, her success was despite her tendency to reject most offers, invitations, and opportunities due to debilitating social anxiety.

She was also uncomfortable with her weight. Apparently being powerful and receiving accolades for her success did not translate into self-love and acceptance.

That's when she came up with the idea to write a book which she called, *A Year of Yes,* during which she would chronicle the results of saying "yes" to everything for a full-365 days.

As much as I like the title, *A Year of Yes*, it's the subtitle that turns me on: *"How to Dance It Out, Stand in the Sun and*

Be Your Own Person." Fuck, I'd love to have come up with that one. Anyway…

In her book, Shonda shares the five key lessons she learned during the year. I have no intention of covering each of them (just go buy the damn book), but I do want to highlight two of them.

Lesson #1 is: *Say "Yes" to Using Your Voice.*

Shonda says she found it easy to give voice to the characters she wrote for her shows, while not being enough to say what she wanted to say in the real world. She decided to speak her mind. It was liberating.

> *"Ditch the dream. Be a doer, not a dreamer."*
>
> -Shonda Rhimes

Lesson #4 is: *Say "Yes" to Love*

This section is heartbreaking. In it, Shonda talks about how she once broke off an engagement with a man who truly loved her out of fear, telling herself marriage was for other people, just not for her.

Did she eventually find love? Fellow authors never read and tell.

Go read the book.

So, showing up is fucking huge—but it's just the first step. The next step is to *do* something.

To get into action.

We're talking work, bitches.

2. Put in the Work.

When it comes to work, no one worked harder than Kobe Bryant.

Bryant wanted to be great and decided to be great. The problem was, he wasn't as naturally talented as many others.

But he didn't feel sorry for himself because his talent wasn't effortless. He committed to working himself to greatness.

Kobe's work ethic was insane. During high school, he showed up at 5 a.m. and didn't leave practice until 7 p.m.—at the end he would often shoot until he made 400 shots. So, it wasn't luck that got him drafted as a high school student straight into the NBA.

It was fucking hard work.

Kobe also knew the importance of maintaining his physical body. He ate right, refusing to eat junk food. He got good sleep, adopted meditation and mindfulness into his daily habits, and never allowed himself to get out of shape during the off-season.

> *"Integrity is doing the right thing, even when no one is watching."*
> -C.S. Lewis

For the 2012 Olympics, Kobe lost 16 pounds to take the pressure off his knees, which he iced for 20 minutes at a time, three times per day. He also did acupuncture.

Like many NBA players, Kobe watched film of himself. Unlike other NBA players, he watched it *during halftime* to improve his performance in the second half.

An NBA scout once wrote: "Allen Iverson loves to play when the lights come on. Kobe loves doing the shit before the lights come on."

And that's the difference, isn't it?

Most of us are willing to show up and do the work when the lights are on us. But are we willing to show up and do the work when the lights are off?

(BTW: Just for the fuck of it, Kobe taught himself to play Beethoven's *Moonlight Sonata*. No lessons. Just by ear. Just because he could.)

Kobe Bryant was a role model for everyone, and his life was tragically short.

Lots of Little Steps

Jim Randel wrote a book called *Skinny on Success* where he researched the careers of 1,000 successful entrepreneurs, musicians, actors, and other such fabulous people. And guess what he found? He found that 99 percent of them didn't have a single big break, even if they pointed to one.

Randel discovered success was a series of little steps, day in and day out, which led to people getting what they wanted. The thing that looked like *the* lucky break only appeared that way. It was simply part of the whole.

So, what work habits does that boss babe CEO you admire possess? We all want her bank account, but what will it take for you to be brave enough to admit you want it, and then do something about it?

You think her good luck is an accident?

Oh, please.

It seems like no one wants to fucking work today. See how far it gets you.

I work my ass off. How can someone with six kids not work their ass off? But I love what I do in this life, so it feels *effortless*. Someone else looking in from the outside might say, *"Wow, Branden does a lot of fucking work."*

When you are on the right vibration with your life, and you have calibrated your energy to live in the version of your highest self, the next step is right there in your face. You just need to have the courage to take it.

Be 10X Bolder.

Nothing makes you look smarter than quoting some shit in Latin, so I wanted to make sure we included this phrase in the book. Here it is:

"Audentes fortuna iuuat."

Loosely translated, it means, "Fortune favors the bold." (Hey, isn't that the same thing Richard Branson said?)

Looked at another way, *"You miss 100 percent of the shots you don't take."* That's from Plato or maybe it was Wayne Gretzky.

I once heard someone ask, "What would you do if you were 10 times bolder?"

Seriously, what would you do?

- *Who would you talk to if you were 10x bolder?*
- *What would you ask for if you were 10x bolder?*

- *What would you attempt if you were 10x bolder?*
- *When would you start if you were 10x bolder?* (Hint: the answer is not next year, or when you *feel* ready.)

What's the secret to being bold? I believe the most important thing is courage.

The First Virtue: Courage

One of the greatest philosophers of all time was a man named Aristotle, who lived 300 years before Christ. As a smart person, he hired Plato to be his life coach.

Aristotle soaked in the knowledge he was taught and decided to become a life coach, too. Phillip II was so impressed by the man, he asked Aristotle to coach Alexander the Great. To be sure, Aristotle was the Tony Robbins of his time.

Before his death, Aristotle created what has become known as the Twelve Virtues, the first of which is courage. When asked why he thought courage was the first virtue, he said:

> **"Courage is the first virtue because it makes all the other virtues possible."**

(For reference, knowledge came in number two.)

I believe Aristotle was one smart dude, and if he says courage is the first virtue, who am I to argue?

What most people get wrong is that they think courage is the absence of fear. It's not. Courage is taking action in the face of fear. Susan Jeffers put it this way when she coined the phrase:

Feel the fear and do it anyway.®

Like most people, I get scared. I feel fear. But I refuse to let it stop me. I do shit, even though I'm scared.

Once I was at an event, and I saw someone I'd always wanted to meet. I found this person very intimidating because he was a best-selling author and highly sought-after success coach. I had a decision to make. I could do nothing or go talk to him. But what would I say?

I stood up, walked over, and asked him who published his books. He gave me the name of his publisher.

The following week, I had another decision to make. Should I pitch my book to his publisher? Again, here I was in the position to approach total strangers. Gulp.

I sent them an email. They wrote back. To my surprise, they wanted to talk.

Now I had to get on the phone with these people and pitch my idea for a book, knowing that rejection was likely because that's what had happened in the past.

"Courage is being scared to death but saddling up anyway."

-John Wayne

I was scared at every step. At every step I was uncertain.

They said no. Which was okay. At least I'd found the courage to pursue the lead.

The next day, the publisher called back. They'd talked it over and had a change of heart. They wanted to publish my book. But there was a catch: They would only do it if I agreed to a two-book deal.

I about fucking fell over.

That first book was *Once Upon a Time, Bitches,* which itself became a best-seller. This book is not my second book with my publisher. It's my fifth.

The Universe doesn't care if you're scared or confident, it only cares that you act. You can wish all you want, but the Universe rewards action. Period.

The funniest part is when people say to me, "Oh, Branden, you're so fearless!" *Fearless my ass.*

Or my favorite: "Wow, Branden, how lucky you are to have gotten your book published." *Luck my ass.*

You want luck to show up in your life? Stop fucking worrying and start doing. Worrying about how you look, or what people might say, is self-defeating. Being defeated is one thing—defeating yourself is another.

If you truly want to create your dream life, get 10x bolder. As Tom Cruise said in *Risky Business,* "Sometimes you gotta say, 'What the fuck,' and make your move."

Pay It Forward.

Nothing goes viral like a story about thirty-eight people in line at a *Chick-fil-A* drive-thru, each of them paying for the person's meal in the car behind them.

At some point, however, the chain must come to an end. There is going to be the *last person* who gets their chicken nuggets for free but doesn't buy any for the person behind them.

That's cool. That's their choice. It doesn't make them a bad person. The truth is if you are doing something because you believe that there's a reward coming your way, you're doing it for the wrong reason. It's about putting out good vibes, good energy, and helping people.

At the same time, understand that karma is real. That's why it's part of the good luck formula. Plus, it's fucking cool to just do something nice for a stranger.

> *"If you want more of anything, get in the habit of giving more of everything."*

If you are looking around and finding a serious lack of luck in your life, let's look at how much you are paying it forward.

You want more likes and comments on your posts? *Start liking and commenting on other people's posts.*

You want people to support your small business? *Terrific. Support other small businesses.*

You want someone to talk to when things are stressful? *Be there for a friend in need.*

You want people to be generous to you? *Be generous.*

You want random cool shit to happen to you? *Do random cool shit for other people.*

You want more luck to show up in your life? *Make someone else feel lucky.*

You want your husband to put his smelly underwear in the hamper? I don't know what the fuck to tell you.

Karma is the Universe's way of saying, *"I saw that, bitch."*

My advice? Do not screw with karma. People who do get their ass kicked.

Tiger Woods has a reputation for being a bad tipper. According to the *Miami Times,* Tiger once took back a $5 tip he'd just given a blackjack dealer when he realized he'd already tipped him—while playing $10,000 a hand.

To be clear: this is not evidence of Tiger's overall lack of generosity. For all we know, he's given millions to charity. Even so, getting petty over $5 is no way to curry favor with the woman upstairs. She remembers shit like that. Can you spell Elin?

Put good stuff out in the Universe and it will get returned to you in ways that you could never have predicted.

Put In Your 10,000 Hours

In his blockbuster book, *Outliers,* Canadian author Malcolm Gladwell presented his thesis that mastery in any area of life requires 10,000 hours of study and intense practice.

For reference, 10,000 hours is only 417 days, assuming you can study and practice 24 hours a day for a year-and-a-half without stopping to eat, sleep, or go to the bathroom.

At 8 hours a day, we're talking 1,250 days. Assuming you took weekends off, it's about 3½ years. If you think this means you can master something in 4 years in college, forget it. For one thing, time in college is spread over multiple topics. For another thing, very few professors are masters at anything other than figuring out how to achieve tenure.

The only thing most college students achieve mastery in is partying.

The realistic amount of time to achieve mastery in most things is approximately 10 years, at 4 hours a day, 5 days a week. Can you spell gymnastics?

Anyone who wants to *go for the gold* needs to be willing to dedicate every moment of free time to the sport. Friends? Forget it unless your friends are fellow gymnasts. Choir? Band? Track? Chess club? Forget it. You want to be great at chess, do chess and forget the parallel bars. One or the other. Pick one. Never both.

It's called sacrifice.

But, Branden, I don't want to be a gymnast. I just want to play the violin. Do you think there is anyone who masters the violin... or becomes a black belt... or becomes a world-class bartender or belly dancer, with less time and devotion? No, there isn't.

"No one gets lucky at anything that really matters. And anything that really matters comes with a price."

Excellence isn't free.

Mastery isn't painless.

Oh, there will be pain.

True success is never quick. It takes years in sweaty gyms and quiet libraries and getting coffee for Quentin Tarantino without pay on the outside chance he takes a liking to you, and you get lucky enough to be hired at minimum wage.

No one gets lucky at anything that matters. And anything that matters always comes at a price.

Pay Now or Pay Later. But You *Will* Pay.

When you were born, you arrived at the inn we call life. Some people get checked into the Ritz Carlton. Others, the Marriott. Or the Holiday Inn, Ramada, or Motel 6. All too many find themselves with no room at all.

Doesn't matter where you stay, there is a bill to be paid. The guy at the front desk wants his money.

Some people have rich families who handle the bill. Even if they trash the place, they'll put it on their card. The rest of us need to get good grades and go to work to pay the price.

If we work hard enough, we get to upgrade to better digs. Others refuse to pay and get downgraded to one of those seedy $99/week places near skid row with the sweaty guy behind the bullet-proof glass, reading a two-year-old copy of Penthouse (an ironic name if ever there was one.) He wants to be paid, too. He's got a baseball bat behind the counter and he's not afraid to use it.

The clean-cut young lady at the Ritz smiles more, and is better trained, and more polite, but don't test her. She's got a direct line to the hotel office and *she's* not afraid to use it.

But make no mistake—regardless of your lodgings, you will pay the price for staying there, whether that is eight years or eighty-eight years from now.

You. Will. Pay.

There will be a price for the room. And the food. And the spa (at the best places) or the laundry room (at the not-so-good places.)

There is a price to be paid for everything: health, relationships, entertainment, clothing, and on and on. And let's not forget cable.

Most people justify their mediocre lodgings by saying life fucked them over. Or they claim there are no rooms for them at the better places. This is a lie.

The truth is, they are simply not willing to pay the price.

You will pay.

One way or the other, *you will pay.*

> *"It doesn't matter where you stay, there is a bill to be paid. The guy at the front desk wants his money."*

The only questions are, will you pay as you go, or all at once, at checkout—in the form of health problems, pain, lack of mobility, poverty, anger, and regret—for not having taken action earlier while you still could, is a bitch, bitches.

> "Luck is a concept invented by the weak to explain their failures."
>
> -Ron Swanson

PART SEVEN

Try. Fail. Try. Fail. Try. Get Lucky.

Few people equate failure with having good luck.

Good Luck = Success

Bad Luck = Failure

Right? Not so fast.

The world is filled with products, inventions, and other discoveries that are a direct result of failed projects and fumbled experiments. For example:

- Jell-O
- Shatterproof glass
- The microwave
- Sony Walkman
- Levi jeans
- Band-Aids
- Kleenex
- Corn Flakes
- Lifesavers
- Pyrex cookware
- Popsicles
- Penicillin
- Silly putty

Each of the above is the direct result of something tried and failed. Even the tires on your car are thanks to Charles Goodyear's fuck-up that led to the discovery of vulcanized rubber.

In 1968, a man named Spencer Silver was tasked with developing the most adhesive glue ever created for use in the construction of airplanes. Rather than creating the strongest adhesive ever, he created a substance so weak it could be peeled away, barely sticking at all. Not only had he failed, he failed spectacularly. (Hey, if you're going to fail, go big, right?)

Fortunately, a co-worker at 3M, a man named Art Fry, heard about the adhesive and thought it might be good for something else.

Fry, who sang in a church choir, was always losing his hymn notes. He applied the adhesive to the back of the paper to see if they could be stuck to the pages of his church songbook and removed without leaving residue.

It worked.

Six years later, Post-It Notes became 3M's most successful new product ever, generating $100 million in sales (this was back in 1985 when $100 million was still a lot of money.)

Sometimes the formula turns out to be:

Bad luck = Success

Serendipity, bitches.

Silicon Valley is a veritable graveyard of mistakes, of things tried and failed. While most of the world does everything it can to avoid failure, Silicon Valley has not only accepted failure as a positive, it has become a rite of passage.

But it hasn't always been this way. For example, consider the origin of the word *sin*.

In Roman times, the term 'sin' was used in archery, which simply meant *to miss the mark*. You aimed your arrow, released it, and the shot either hit the target or it missed—being a sin.

In archery, if you sin often enough, you get better and go to the Olympics. In religion, if you sin too much, you go to hell.

"Mis-takes" in Hollywood

Nowhere in the world are mistakes more common than in Hollywood. This is where the word mistakes came from, a combination of two words:

Mis + Takes

In Hollywood, when an actor screws up their lines, what do they do? The director yells, *"Cut!"* and then they do the *take* over again.

And again.

And again.

Until they finally get it right. *Mis-takes* are so acceptable in Hollywood now, they show the mistakes (also known as, outtakes) during the end credits of many movies. They even post the outtakes to YouTube. Mistakes are part of the entertainment!

Speaking of movies, here's a little quiz.

What do the following famous lines from these Hollywood movies have in common?

- Leonardo DiCaprio declaring, "I'm the king of the world!" in *Titanic*.
- Jack Nicholson saying, "Here's Johnny!" in *The Shining*.
- Matthew McConaughey saying, "All right, All right, All right," in *Dazed and Confused*.
- "You're going to need a bigger boat," from *Jaws*.
- Jack Nicholson (again) telling Tom Cruise, "You can't handle the truth!" in *A Few Good Men*.

Give up? The answer is none of these lines were in the script. They are all the result of an actor being willing to try something and go *off-script*. In every case, the actor ran the risk of failure, or at a minimum, embarrassment. Then again, maybe not. Maybe there was no risk at all. Maybe going off-script and even screwing up is an expectation.

These actors weren't "lucky" to get great lines. They made them up and they *spoke them* into existence. They took a chance.

As kids, we weren't fazed at all when we screwed up or made mistakes. We shrugged it off. We laughed when we fucked up. But then, when we got older, our willingness to try and fail gets lost, usually because parents and teachers told us failing was bad and to be avoided.

Before you know it, our sense of adventure is replaced with fear. Fear of failure. Fear of embarrassment. Fear of rejection. Fear of fucking up.

The irony is that, in our attempt to avoid failure, we miss out on the serendipitous good luck that might have come our way.

Have you considered that, if you are not currently experiencing much good luck, it might just be due to your fear of experiencing failure or embarrassing yourself?

Will You Come to the Bathroom with Me?

Now we need to talk about my ass, thighs, and stomach for a bit. I know, WTF do they have to do with luck? To be honest, not much. But they're the beneficiary of someone taking a chance and someone who said, "Fuck luck."

I'm talking about a product called *Spanx*, created by a woman named Sara Blakely.

When Sara started her entrepreneurial journey, she'd never taken a business class or worked in fashion or retail. She had a full-time job and $5,000 in savings. That's it.

But she had an idea for a product. Something that would flatter a woman's figure but was not your typical old-fashioned girdle; think pantyhose, but without feet.

Even though she didn't have a product yet, Sara knew she was onto something and wanted to protect her idea. She needed a patent.

Sara went from attorney to attorney, but none of them got it. One attorney found the idea was so bizarre, he thought maybe he was on *Candid Camera*. Undeterred, she decided to write the patent herself. Then, she ran into a ton of rejection just trying to get someone to make the prototype. This took her a year of working nights and weekends. Finally, she had a tangible product she could pitch.

After a lot of dead ends, Sara found out how to reach the hosiery buyer for Neiman Marcus in Dallas, Texas. She called over and over, trying different times on different days until eventually, a woman picked up. It took some convincing, but the woman said if Sara was willing to get on a plane and fly to their offices in Dallas, she'd see her.

With the prototype of her product in a Ziplock bag, and with nothing but a color photocopy of the art for the packaging, Sara headed to Dallas.

Five minutes in, Sara could tell the meeting was not going well. She knew she needed to do something dramatic. Sara said, *"I know this may sound a little weird, but would you please come with me to the bathroom? I want to show you how my product works, before and after."*

The woman hesitated, then agreed.

The demonstration worked.

The buyer said, *"I'm going to put your product in seven stores, and we'll see how it goes."*

The rest is history.

Today, Spanx is a household name, and Sara Blakely is a billionaire. Why? Four reasons:

1. She had a good idea.
2. She did the work.
3. She was willing to look stupid and maybe fail.
4. She said, "Fuck luck."

And that's the problem. Most of us have good ideas from time to time. But what do we do with them? Not a damn thing. And we count on luck to pull us through.

Growth is the Result Dis-Comfort.

One of my favorite stories is about the critical role struggle plays in personal growth.

One day, while hiking in the woods, a man finds a cocoon with a butterfly inside, struggling to get out and spread its wings. Fascinated, the man sat down to watch, eager to witness one of nature's miracles.

For several hours the man watched as the butterfly struggled to force its body through a small opening in the cocoon.

But it just didn't seem to be able to do it.

The man had an idea. He took a pair of scissors and carefully enlarged the hole in the cocoon. And it worked. Within minutes it emerged. But something was wrong.

For some reason, the butterfly didn't unfurl its wings as the man expected. And it was oddly shaped. The body looked big and swollen, and the wings were small and shriveled.

In his attempt at kindness, the man did not realize that struggling to get through the small opening of the cocoon was nature's way of forcing fluid from the body of the butterfly into its wings. By removing the butterfly's need to struggle, he had robbed it of what it needed to do to grow.

It's the same for us. In our ever-present quest for comfort and safety, we rob ourselves of the opportunity to struggle and grow.

Now, I know what you're probably thinking: Thanks for the cool story, Branden, but what in the fuck does this have to do with luck? Glad you asked.

Think about this for a moment, and be completely honest: When was the last time you achieved something big, something you were truly proud of, while you were on your sofa, in the safety of your living room, watching Netflix and chowing down on a bag of Cheetos? Here, let me help you out.

The answer is never.

Good luck doesn't come knocking on your door. It shows up because of hard work and proactive effort. Comfort and safety come at a cost, and that cost is lost potential.

You want more good luck to show up in your life? Get to work. What's inexcusable is to fail due to inaction.

What have you failed at today? What did you fuck up at yesterday? Nothing? You may think that was a good day. It wasn't. It was a fucking bad day—a day in which your chances of something great happening was virtually zero.

Good luck is attracted to hard work. Good luck is attracted to a willingness to risk. The Universe rewards action. Fortune favors the bold.

You wanna know what the comfort zone really is?

It is the No-Luck Zone.

"Bad luck either destroys you or makes you the man or woman you really are."

-Amitabh Bachahan

FINAL THOUGHTS

Be Careful What You Wish For

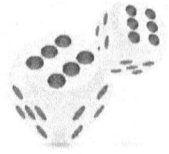

What's the number one thing people wish for? You guessed it. They want to win the lottery. And why is this the thing people wish for most? Because it doesn't require work. Just luck.

If you're here on page 104 and you still think this is how it works, then I've failed. Sorry about that. $12.95 down the drain. Go write a review and bitch about it.

But I haven't failed, have I?

No.

You know luck is not a plan. You've known it all along. Only fools place their future on the luck of the draw. And you're no fool. Besides, winning the lottery isn't really what it's cracked up to be. Take Jack Whittaker, for example.

It's Christmas morning, 2002, and Andrew "Jack" Whittaker has just won, to that point, the largest amount awarded to a single Powerball ticket holder ever. $314.9 million. $113 million in a lump sum after tax. Nice Christmas. It probably snowed, too.

Unlike lots of lottery winners, Jack wasn't selfish. He set up a charitable foundation, donated money to build a church in West Virginia, and bought a house and car for the woman who sold him the winning ticket.

Unfortunately, the big win was big news.

Someone stole half a million dollars from his car (stupidity + bad luck.) Then he was robbed. Another $100,000 gone.

Then random people started suing him for money. Most of the lawsuits were frivolous, but millions more of his fortune went to legal fees. He started drinking (understandable) and offering women money to sleep with him (not so understandable.) His wife divorced him (understandable again.)

To quote Jack: "I wish I'd torn up that ticket."

Jack Whitaker's story is not uncommon.

Dishwasher, Curtis Sharp, Jr. won a $5 million jackpot, and started living large and partying hard—big houses, flashy cars, yadda, yadda, yadda. He left his wife for a lover, and she divorced him (shock.) Eventually, he ran out of money and had to borrow money from his first wife to pay the bills.

Well, there's always going to be a bad story or two, Branden. These are sad exceptions. Okay, let's check the headlines:

William Post III won $16.2 million in the Pennsylvania Lottery, and his brother hired a hitman to kill him so he would inherit the money.

Abraham Shakespeare won $40 million and was murdered for his money.

Marie Holmes won $127 million and was immediately sued by her former fiancé. She was also sued by a local pastor who felt she owed it to God to donate 10 percent of her winnings to the church.

Billy Bob Harrell Jr. won $30 million and committed suicide 2 years later.

...Jeffrey Dampier, Jr. won $20 million and was murdered for it.

But none of this would happen to you, right?

Are you sure?

With or without these horror stories, I can honestly say I'm glad I haven't won the lottery. I used to be that person who wished I could win, but I don't buy tickets anymore. And I wonder: *Who would I have become if I'd won all that money?* I certainly wouldn't be doing the work I'm doing, and not just because I could simply have fun and fuck off. It's because I wouldn't have experienced the struggle of life that has led me to the life I have. A life I love.

Much of the time we're asking the Universe for the wrong thing. When we wish for money, or success, or fame, is that what we really want? No. We want the things that we think money and success and fame will give us.

Peace.

Love.

Happiness.

Meaning.

None of these require money. Or success. Or fame.

We can have peace by deciding to be peaceful. We can have love by deciding to be loving. We can have happiness by deciding to be happy and spread happiness. We can have meaning by deciding to be meaningful to others.

Don't get me wrong:

I want all the things everyone wants. I want money. At a minimum, money makes life easier. And a lot of it can open doors that are otherwise locked to those without it.

And I want more success.

And I wouldn't mind a bit of fame.

But I refuse to wait for any of this to make me feel whole and content and worthy.

My whole-hearted intention for this book was for you to get sick and tired of your own shit and understand that you are more than the thoughts you hold onto. You are more than the shame you embrace. You are more than the pain that has come to you in the past. You are more than someone else's opinion of you.

When I started writing fiction, I did it because I wanted to make money. Then I realized I had something more important to share, I had a voice, and I wanted to use it.

What's interesting is, the money showed up anyway.

I never believed people when they said that if you do what you love that the money would follow. But it's real. It's true.

I have created a life I love. Does that make me lucky?

No.

I decided to fuck luck a long time ago.

Now It's Your Turn

If you find yourself: *Waking up to a life you hate... Looking in the mirror and not liking what you see... Allowing your past to dictate your future... Struggling to make ends meet... Going to bed at the end of the day with a sense of hopelessness...*

Well, fuck that shit.

- This is the only life you've got.

- Hating yourself won't make you thinner or prettier or more desirable.
- Regretting what you did or didn't do eleven years ago won't change anything.
- You are never going to solve your financial problem in a state of fear.
- And fuck feeling helpless and hopeless—the truth is, you are neither.

And, dear motherfucking God, quit counting on luck to turn things around for you. And stop looking for it. Luck isn't found, it's made.

Go out and make some!

About the Author...

BRANDEN LANETTE doesn't look like a typical author, but she has long ignored what she "should" do, say and look like. On her own at a very young age, Branden eventually found herself with the wrong guy, the wrong job, and a bleak future. The fairytale promised as a child never materialized.

Branden realized she wanted something different for her life and realized no one was going to do it for her.

Prince charming wasn't coming to save her—she'd have to save herself. Step-by-step, decision by decision, through major trials and tribulations, Branden learned how to turn heartbreak into happiness and self-judgment into inner joy.

In 2019, Branden had her first book published, *Once Upon a Time, Bitches* followed by two workbooks in 2020, *The Dream Big Bitches Vision Book* and *The Dream Big Bitches Weekly Goal Setting Journal*. In early 2021 she co-authored the book, *Smart Bitches Buy Bitcoin* and is now over the moon for this one, her fifth.

Branden LaNette is an entrepreneur, motivational speaker, coach, wife, and stay-at-home mom.

Through Branden's Radical Activation and Attraction Method, she is helping men and women take control of their destinies, step into their full potential, and conquer the limiting beliefs that have been holding them back so they can live a life they love.

Branden's First Book...

Prince Charming doesn't exist, the Fairy Godmother is drunk, and glass slippers don't come two-day Prime shipping from Amazon. Branden will tell you what to do about it.

"The self-help book I didn't know I needed"... "A gem in the massive rock pile of self-help"... "Funny, cute, and as real as it gets"... these are just a few things said about Branden's first book.

What happened to the fairytale you were promised? No more whining and no more damsel locked in a tower, bullsh*t. Is it possible to design a fairytale life? Control your destiny? Be the hero in your story? Branden thinks there is, and she wants to help you.

Available at Amazon.com.

The "Dream Big, Bitches" Vision Book...

Want to implement everything you've just been inspired to change? This is the workbook you need to do it!

The Dream Big, Bitches Vision Book provides a super fun framework to achieve your wants and desires by getting all the stuff floating in your mind on paper and then turning those visions into realities.

In the same "hold-nothing-back, in-your-face style" as the book, this easy-to-use 8.5 x 11 workbook helps you craft concrete visions for achieving your dream life using a proven step-by-step process designed by Branden.

Available at Amazon.com.

...and the "Dream Big" Goal Setting Journal!

This 52-week "start-any-date you want journal" helps you organize your goals and dreams into actual real-world action steps for achievement.

The large 8.5 by 11 format provides plenty of space to identify your goals and the action steps for achieving them. Also includes Branden's "Thought for the Week" to keep you inspired during your journey.

These guides are designed to work together to help you make the next 52 weeks of your life the best ever!

Available at Amazon.com.

Let's Connect, Bitches!

Facebook: Branden.Lanette

Instagram: @Brandenlanettel

Twitter: @Branden_LaNette

Oh, don't forget, visit me at:

OnceUponATimeBitches.com

Finally... Thank you so much for reading.
You are part of my dream come true.

Is now an okay time to ask for a favor?

I would LOVE and greatly appreciate it if you would consider leaving an honest review of my book on your favorite book-buying platform.